Mastering Your Money: The P.A.T.H. Playbook for Financial Empowerment

Author: Lee Vincent

Copyright 2023 @LeeVincent

ISBN: 9798390210024
Imprint: Independently published

Introduction

Congratulations! You have taken the first step towards financial empowerment by purchasing this book. This playbook is designed to help you achieve your financial goals and take control of your finances. With the P.A.T.H. Playbook, you will learn how to assess your current financial situation, set clear financial goals, create a plan to achieve them, track your progress, and cultivate a positive mindset towards money.

This playbook is the result of my own personal journey with financial management. As someone with a background in business, I have always been interested in money management. However, like many others, I struggled with maintaining wealth and reaching my financial goals. Over the past 10 years, I have researched and experimented with different financial management strategies, and this playbook is the culmination of my efforts.

I have personally used and applied this playbook to my own finances and goals, and it has worked for me one hundred percent. It has helped me to not only maintain wealth but also to grow it. And now, I want to share this playbook with you to help you achieve your own financial success.

In this playbook, you will find a step-by-step guide to managing your finances, setting clear financial goals, and cultivating a positive mindset towards money. The playbook is divided into five sections: Personal Finance Assessment, Action Plan, Tracking and Analysis, Habits and Mindset, and Bonus Section: Resources and Inspiration.

Through a series of prompts and exercises, you will learn how to assess your current financial situation, identify areas for improvement, and create a plan to achieve your financial goals. You will also learn how to cultivate positive financial habits, such as saving money and avoiding debt, and develop a growth mindset towards money through gratitude, affirmations, and visualization.

I am confident that this playbook will help you achieve your financial goals and empower you to take control of your finances. So, let's begin this journey towards financial empowerment together!

---◇---

Building wealth is not a sprint, it's a marathon.

---◇---

Overview

The P.A.T.H. playbook is designed to provide you with a comprehensive guide to achieving financial empowerment. The acronym stands for Personal Finance Assessment, Action Plan, Tracking and Analysis, Habits and Mindset, and Bonus Section: Resources and Inspiration. By following the steps outlined in this playbook, you can gain a better understanding of your current financial situation, set clear financial goals, develop positive financial habits, and cultivate a growth mindset towards money.

The playbook begins with a Personal Finance Assessment, which will help you assess your current financial situation and identify areas for improvement. You'll learn how to analyze your income, expenses, and assets, and create a plan to achieve financial stability.

Next, the Action Plan section will guide you through the process of setting clear financial goals, prioritizing them, and creating a budget to track your progress. You'll also learn how to adjust your plan based on your analysis and stay motivated throughout your financial journey.

The Tracking and Analysis section will help you keep track of your income, expenses, and progress towards your financial goals. By analyzing your data, you'll be able to identify areas for improvement and adjust your plan accordingly.

The Habits and Mindset section will help you develop positive financial habits and cultivate a positive mindset towards money. You'll learn how to save money, avoid debt, and surround yourself with supportive people who share your financial goals and values.

Finally, the Bonus Section: Resources and Inspiration provides additional resources, such as books, websites, or podcasts, for further education and inspiration. You'll also find motivational quotes and success stories to keep you inspired and motivated on your financial journey.

Disclaimer:

The P.A.T.H. Playbook is designed to provide guidance and support for individuals seeking to improve their financial management skills and achieve their financial goals. However, the information provided in this playbook is not intended to be a substitute for professional financial advice.

The author and publisher of this playbook do not assume any liability for the information, advice, or recommendations contained in this playbook. Readers should seek the advice of a professional financial advisor before making any significant financial decisions.

The content provided in this playbook is intended to be informative and educational, but it is not a guarantee of any financial outcomes or results. The information provided in this playbook is subject to change without notice and may not be accurate, complete, or up-to-date.

The reader assumes full responsibility for the use of the information and content provided in this playbook. The author and publisher disclaim any liability for any loss, injury, or damage resulting from the use or application of the information and content provided in this playbook.

P.A.T.H.

Personal Finance Assessment

- Assess your current financial situation.
- Identify your income, expenses, and assets
- Analyze your financial data to identify areas for improvement.

Action Plan

- Set clear financial goals.
- Prioritize your goals and create a plan to achieve them.
- Create a budget and track your progress towards your goals.

Tracking and Analysis

- Track your income, expenses, and progress towards your financial goals.
- Analyze your data to identify areas for improvement.
- Adjust your plan accordingly based on your analysis.

Habits and Mindset

- Develop positive financial habits, such as saving money and avoiding debt.
- Cultivate a positive mindset towards money through gratitude, affirmations, and visualization
- Surround yourself with supportive people who share your financial goals and values.

Part 1: Personal Finance Assessment

To create a Personal Finance Assessment, you will need to consider the following elements:

1. Income: Determine your monthly income, including your salary or wages, investment income, and any other sources of income.
2. Expenses: Identify all of your monthly expenses, including fixed expenses (rent or mortgage payments, car payments, insurance, utilities) and variable expenses (groceries, dining out, entertainment).
3. Debt: Determine the amount of debt you owe, including credit cards, loans, and any other debts.
4. Assets: Identify your assets, including your home, car, investments, and any other valuable possessions.
5. Savings: Determine how much money you have in savings and investments.
6. Financial Goals: Identify your short-term and long-term financial goals, such as paying off debt, saving for retirement, or buying a house.
7. Financial Habits: Evaluate your financial habits, such as spending and saving habits, to identify areas for improvement.

By considering these elements, you can create a comprehensive Personal Finance Assessment that will provide you with a clear picture of your current financial situation and help you identify areas for improvement.

Guide to using the Personal Finance Assessment in the planner:

1. Gather all necessary information: Before you start using the Personal Finance Assessment, make sure you have all the necessary information on hand. This includes your income, expenses, debts, assets, savings, and financial goals.
2. Input your financial information: Use the planner to input your financial information under each corresponding element, including income, expenses, debt, assets, and savings.
3. Analyze your financial data: Once you've input all your financial information, use the planner to analyze your data. Look at your income and expenses to determine if you're living within your means. Evaluate your debt to determine if you need to make any changes to your repayment plan. Look at your assets and savings to determine if you're on track to meet your financial goals.
4. Identify areas for improvement: Based on your analysis, identify areas for improvement in your finances. This could include reducing expenses, paying off debt, increasing savings, or setting new financial goals.
5. Create an action plan: Once you've identified areas for improvement, create an action plan to address them. Prioritize your goals and create a plan to achieve them, such as reducing expenses or increasing savings.
6. Track your progress: Use the planner to track your progress towards your financial goals. Regularly update your financial information and adjust your plan accordingly based on your analysis.

PERSONAL FINANCE ASSESSMENT

DATE:	

SALARY		RENT EXPENSE/MORTGAGE	
BUSINESS		UTILITIES EXPENSES Electric/Water/Telephone/Internet	
OTHER SOURCES		FOOD	
OTHER SOURCES		INSURANCE	
TOTAL INCOME		INTEREST EXPENSE/INSURANCE	
NET MONTHLY INCOME Total Income - Total Expenses		TOTAL EXPENSES	

ASSETS

Particular	Amount
Savings:	
Investment	
Total Assets	

Saving Habits:
_____
_____
_____

Short-term Financial Goals:
_____
_____
_____

DEBTS

Particular	Amount
Credit Card	
Credit Card	
Loans	
Loans	
Others	
Total Debt	

Spending Habits:
_____
_____
_____

Areas for Improvement:
_____
_____
_____

Long-term Financial Goals:
_____
_____
_____

Part 2: Action Plan

The Action Plan section of the P.A.T.H. playbook is designed to help you set clear financial goals and create a plan to achieve them. The section is divided into three parts: setting financial goals, prioritizing goals, and creating a budget.

The first part, setting financial goals, is about identifying what you want to achieve financially. It could be buying a house, paying off debt, saving for retirement, or any other financial goal you have in mind. The goal should be specific, measurable, achievable, relevant, and time-bound. You will learn how to set SMART goals and create an action plan for each goal.

The second part of the Action Plan is prioritizing goals. Once you have identified your financial goals, you need to prioritize them based on their importance. You will learn how to use the Eisenhower Matrix to prioritize your goals and create a plan to achieve them.

The third part is creating a budget. A budget is a powerful tool that helps you track your income and expenses, and make sure that you are on track to achieve your financial goals. You will learn how to create a budget, track your expenses, and make adjustments if necessary. You will also learn how to use a financial planner to monitor your progress towards your financial goals.

Action Planner Outline:

1. Clear Financial Goals: This section should prompt you to set clear, specific, and measurable financial goals. These goals should align with your overall financial objectives, such as paying off debt, saving for a down payment on a house, or building an emergency fund.

   It is also vital to set first your values or priorities before finalizing your goal. Values are essential in goal setting because they serve as the foundation of our motivation and desires. When we set goals that are aligned with our values, we are more likely to feel a sense of purpose and fulfillment in achieving them.

   For example, if one of our core values is family, setting a goal to spend more quality time with our loved ones may be highly motivating for us. On the other hand, if our goal is to earn a large amount of money but it goes against our values of honesty and integrity, we may find ourselves feeling unfulfilled and lacking in motivation.

2. Prioritization of Goals: Once you've identified your financial goals, prioritize them based on their importance and urgency. This section should help you understand which goals should take precedence and which ones can wait.
3. Action Steps: After prioritizing your goals, create an action plan to achieve them. Break down each goal into smaller, actionable steps, and include deadlines and milestones to help you stay on track.

4. Budgeting: This section should help you create a budget that aligns with your financial goals. This includes tracking your income, expenses, and savings, and identifying areas where you can cut back to save money.
5. Progress Tracking: To stay motivated and on track towards your financial goals, it's essential to track your progress regularly. This section should prompt you to track your progress towards your goals and adjust your action plan if necessary.
6. Reflection and Analysis: Periodically reviewing your progress is essential to ensure that you are on track towards achieving your financial goals. This section should prompt you to reflect on your progress, analyze any setbacks or successes, and make any necessary adjustments to your plan.

By including these elements in the Action Plan Planner, you can create a clear plan to achieve your financial goals and track your progress towards financial freedom.

Overall, the Action Plan section of the P.A.T.H. playbook provides a structured approach to managing your finances and achieving your financial goals. It helps you set clear financial goals, prioritize them, and create a budget to achieve them. With the P.A.T.H. playbook, you will have a clear roadmap to financial freedom and success.

The Action Planner in this playbook begins with your annual action plan, The Action Planner included in this playbook begins with an annual action plan where you can set your major goal and then break it down into the number of months you need to achieve it. You will then write specific goals for each month to help you break down your major goal into achievable bits. The next planner is for your monthly goal, which will be further broken down into weekly goals. where you set your major financial goal and then break it down into smaller, achievable goals for each month. This approach allows you to divide your major goal into manageable pieces and work towards them steadily throughout the year. By setting specific monthly goals, you can track your progress towards your major goal and adjust your plan accordingly.

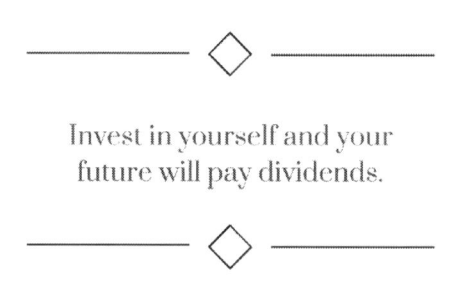

Invest in yourself and your future will pay dividends.

Action Planner

GOAL	START DATE:	DUE DATE:

Your Values
What are the things that are most important to you?

Your Vision
What is your long-term goal?

BUDGET

POSSIBLE OBSTACLES AND HOW TO OVERCOME THEM:

GOAL PROGRESS: 0% ☐☐☐☐☐☐☐☐☐☐ 100%

SPECIFIC GOALS

Month 1	Month 7
Month 2	Month 8
Month 3	Month 9
Month 4	Month 10
Month 5	Month 11
Month 6	Month 12

Action Plan

MONTHLY GOAL	START DATE:	DUE DATE:

SPECIFIC GOAL
Your goal for the month

SPECIFIC GOAL
Additional goal for the month if any

NOTES OF GRATITUDE
Gratitude writing conditions your mind to be more goal-oriented.

URGENT TASKS

GOAL PROGRESS: 0%   100%

WEEKLY PLAN

Week 1

Week 2

Week 3

Month 4

NOTES	SPECIAL DATES
BUDGET & RESOURCES	SUPPORT GROUP

Action Plan

MONTHLY GOAL	START DATE:	DUE DATE:

SPECIFIC GOAL
Your goal for the month

SPECIFIC GOAL
Additional goal for the month if any

NOTES OF GRATITUDE
Gratitude writing conditions your mind to be more goal-oriented.

URGENT TASKS

GOAL PROGRESS:　0%　☐ ☐ ☐ ☐　100%

WEEKLY PLAN

Week 1

Week 2

Week 3

Month 4

NOTES	SPECIAL DATES
BUDGET & RESOURCES	SUPPORT GROUP

Action Plan

MONTHLY GOAL | START DATE: | DUE DATE:

SPECIFIC GOAL
Your goal for the month

SPECIFIC GOAL
Additional goal for the month if any

NOTES OF GRATITUDE
Gratitude writing conditions your mind to be more goal-oriented.

URGENT TASKS

GOAL PROGRESS: 0% ☐ ☐ ☐ ☐ 100%

WEEKLY PLAN

Week 1

Week 2

Week 3

Month 4

NOTES	SPECIAL DATES
BUDGET & RESOURCES	**SUPPORT GROUP**

Action Plan

| MONTHLY GOAL | START DATE: | DUE DATE: |

SPECIFIC GOAL
Your goal for the month

SPECIFIC GOAL
Additional goal for the month if any

NOTES OF GRATITUDE
Gratitude writing conditions your mind to be more goal-oriented.

URGENT TASKS

GOAL PROGRESS: 0% ▢ ▢ ▢ ▢ 100%

WEEKLY PLAN

Week 1

Week 2

Week 3

Month 4

NOTES	SPECIAL DATES
BUDGET & RESOURCES	SUPPORT GROUP

Action Plan

| MONTHLY GOAL | START DATE: | DUE DATE: |

SPECIFIC GOAL
Your goal for the month

SPECIFIC GOAL
Additional goal for the month if any

NOTES OF GRATITUDE
Gratitude writing conditions your mind to be more goal-oriented.

URGENT TASKS

GOAL PROGRESS: 0% ☐ ☐ ☐ ☐ 100%

WEEKLY PLAN

Week 1

Week 2

Week 3

Month 4

NOTES	SPECIAL DATES
BUDGET & RESOURCES	SUPPORT GROUP

Action Plan

| MONTHLY GOAL | START DATE: | DUE DATE: |

SPECIFIC GOAL
Your goal for the month

SPECIFIC GOAL
Additional goal for the month if any

NOTES OF GRATITUDE
Gratitude writing conditions your mind to be more goal-oriented.

URGENT TASKS

GOAL PROGRESS: 0% □ □ □ □   100%

WEEKLY PLAN

Week 1

Week 2

Week 3

Month 4

| NOTES | SPECIAL DATES |

| BUDGET & RESOURCES | SUPPORT GROUP |

Action Plan

MONTHLY GOAL | START DATE: | DUE DATE:

SPECIFIC GOAL
Your goal for the month

SPECIFIC GOAL
Additional goal for the month if any

NOTES OF GRATITUDE
Gratitude writing conditions your mind to be more goal-oriented.

URGENT TASKS

GOAL PROGRESS: 0% | | | | 100%

WEEKLY PLAN

Week 1

Week 2

Week 3

Month 4

NOTES | SPECIAL DATES

BUDGET & RESOURCES | SUPPORT GROUP

Action Plan

| MONTHLY GOAL | START DATE: | DUE DATE: |

SPECIFIC GOAL
Your goal for the month

SPECIFIC GOAL
Additional goal for the month if any

NOTES OF GRATITUDE
Gratitude writing conditions your mind to be more goal-oriented.

URGENT TASKS

GOAL PROGRESS: 0% □□□□ 100%

WEEKLY PLAN

Week 1

Week 2

Week 3

Month 4

| NOTES | SPECIAL DATES |

| BUDGET & RESOURCES | SUPPORT GROUP |

Action Plan

| MONTHLY GOAL | START DATE: | DUE DATE: |

SPECIFIC GOAL
Your goal for the month

SPECIFIC GOAL
Additional goal for the month if any

NOTES OF GRATITUDE
Gratitude writing conditions your mind to be more goal-oriented.

URGENT TASKS

GOAL PROGRESS: 0%   [ ][ ][ ][ ]   100%

WEEKLY PLAN

Week 1

Week 2

Week 3

Month 4

| NOTES | SPECIAL DATES |

| BUDGET & RESOURCES | SUPPORT GROUP |

Action Plan

| MONTHLY GOAL | START DATE: | DUE DATE: |

SPECIFIC GOAL
Your goal for the month

SPECIFIC GOAL
Additional goal for the month if any

NOTES OF GRATITUDE
Gratitude writing conditions your mind to be more goal-oriented.

URGENT TASKS

GOAL PROGRESS: 0% ☐ ☐ ☐ ☐ 100%

WEEKLY PLAN

Week 1

Week 2

Week 3

Month 4

NOTES	SPECIAL DATES
BUDGET & RESOURCES	SUPPORT GROUP

Action Plan

MONTHLY GOAL	START DATE:	DUE DATE:

SPECIFIC GOAL
Your goal for the month

SPECIFIC GOAL
Additional goal for the month if any

NOTES OF GRATITUDE
Gratitude writing conditions your mind to be more goal-oriented.

URGENT TASKS

GOAL PROGRESS: 0% [ ][ ][ ][ ] 100%

WEEKLY PLAN

Week 1

Week 2

Week 3

Month 4

NOTES	SPECIAL DATES
BUDGET & RESOURCES	SUPPORT GROUP

Action Plan

MONTHLY GOAL | START DATE: | DUE DATE:

SPECIFIC GOAL
Your goal for the month

SPECIFIC GOAL
Additional goal for the month if any

NOTES OF GRATITUDE
Gratitude writing conditions your mind to be more goal-oriented.

URGENT TASKS

GOAL PROGRESS: 0% ☐ ☐ ☐ ☐ 100%

WEEKLY PLAN

Week 1

Week 2

Week 3

Month 4

NOTES	SPECIAL DATES
BUDGET & RESOURCES	SUPPORT GROUP

Part 3: Tracking and Analysis

Welcome to the Tracking and Analysis section of the P.A.T.H. Playbook. This section is all about monitoring your progress towards your financial goals and making adjustments along the way. It provides a framework for tracking your income, expenses, and progress towards your financial goals on a regular basis.

By tracking your finances, you gain a clear understanding of where your money is going and how it is contributing to your overall financial picture. This information allows you to identify areas where you can improve and make changes to better align with your financial goals.

The Tracking and Analysis form is a powerful tool that can help you achieve financial success by providing a clear picture of your finances and progress towards your goals. We hope that you find this section helpful in achieving financial freedom and creating the life you desire.

Guide for using the Tracking and Analysis Sheet:

1. Record the monthly totals of the Personal Finance Assessment in the sheet.
2. Monitor the values and analyze if you are hitting your goal in your action planner.

Guide for using the Monthly Personal Finance Assessment:

1. Start by recording your income: List down all sources of income, including your salary, freelance work, or any other means of earning money. You may choose to break down your income into categories such as primary and secondary sources.
2. Record your expenses: List all your expenses, including rent/mortgage payments, utilities, groceries, transportation, entertainment, and any other regular or occasional expenses. Be as specific as possible and break down your expenses into categories to make it easier to analyze later.
3. Set a budget: Based on your income and expenses, create a budget that includes all the necessary expenses and allows for savings and investments. Make sure to set realistic goals and track your progress regularly.
4. Track your expenses regularly: Keep track of your expenses daily or weekly by recording all purchases and payments made. This will help you stay within your budget and identify areas where you may be overspending.
5. Analyze your data: After a month or so, analyze your income and expenses data to identify areas for improvement. Look for patterns, such as overspending on certain categories, and adjust your budget accordingly.
6. Adjust your plan: Based on your analysis, adjust your budget and spending habits to meet your financial goals. Be flexible and open to changes as your financial situation may change over time.
7. Regularly update your Tracking and Analysis Sheet: Keep updating your income and expenses regularly to stay on top of your finances and monitor your progress towards your financial goals.

By using the Tracking and Analysis Sheet regularly, you can gain a better understanding of your finances and make informed decisions about your money. It can also help you identify areas for improvement and make adjustments to meet your financial goals.

Tracking and Analysis Sheet

Month	Total Asset	Total Debts	Net Income	Investment	Total Savings
1					
2					
3					
4					
5					
6					
7					
8					
9					
10					
11					
12					
TOTAL					

Reflection and Adjustments

Urgent Adjustments:

"Wealth is not about having a lot of money; it's about having a lot of options." - Chris Rock

PERSONAL FINANCE ASSESSMENT

DATE:	

SALARY		RENT EXPENSE/MORTGAGE	
BUSINESS		UTILITIES EXPENSES Electric/Water/Telephone/Internet	
OTHER SOURCES		FOOD	
OTHER SOURCES		INSURANCE	
TOTAL INCOME		INTEREST EXPENSE/INSURANCE	
NET MONTHLY INCOME Total Income - Total Expenses		TOTAL EXPENSES	

ASSETS

Particular	Amount

Savings:

Investment

Total Assets

Saving Habits:

Short-term Financial Goals:

DEBTS

Particular	Amount
Credit Card	
Credit Card	
Loans	
Loans	
Others	
Total Debt	

Spending Habits:

Areas for Improvement:

Long-term Financial Goals:

PERSONAL FINANCE ASSESSMENT

DATE:

SALARY		RENT EXPENSE/MORTGAGE	
BUSINESS		UTILITIES EXPENSES Electric/Water/Telephone/Internet	
OTHER SOURCES		FOOD	
OTHER SOURCES		INSURANCE	
TOTAL INCOME		INTEREST EXPENSE/INSURANCE	
NET MONTHLY INCOME Total Income - Total Expenses		TOTAL EXPENSES	

ASSETS

Particular	Amount

Savings:

Investment

Total Assets

Saving Habits:

Short-term Financial Goals:

DEBTS

Particular	Amount
Credit Card	
Credit Card	
Loans	
Loans	
Others	
Total Debt	

Spending Habits:

Areas for Improvement:

Long-term Financial Goals:

PERSONAL FINANCE ASSESSMENT

DATE:	

SALARY	RENT EXPENSE/MORTGAGE
BUSINESS	UTILITIES EXPENSES Electric/Water/Telephone/Internet
OTHER SOURCES	FOOD
OTHER SOURCES	INSURANCE
TOTAL INCOME	INTEREST EXPENSE/INSURANCE
NET MONTHLY INCOME Total Income - Total Expenses	TOTAL EXPENSES

ASSETS

Particular	Amount
Savings:	
Investment	
Total Assets	

DEBTS

Particular	Amount
Credit Card	
Credit Card	
Loans	
Loans	
Others	
Total Debt	

Spending Habits:

Saving Habits:

Areas for Improvement:

Short-term Financial Goals:

Long-term Financial Goals:

PERSONAL FINANCE ASSESSMENT

DATE:

SALARY		RENT EXPENSE/MORTGAGE	
BUSINESS		UTILITIES EXPENSES Electric/Water/Telephone/Internet	
OTHER SOURCES		FOOD	
OTHER SOURCES		INSURANCE	
TOTAL INCOME		INTEREST EXPENSE/INSURANCE	
NET MONTHLY INCOME Total Income - Total Expenses		TOTAL EXPENSES	

ASSETS

Particular	Amount
Savings:	
Investment	
Total Assets	

Saving Habits:

DEBTS

Particular	Amount
Credit Card	
Credit Card	
Loans	
Loans	
Others	
Total Debt	

Spending Habits:

Areas for Improvement:

Short-term Financial Goals:

Long-term Financial Goals:

PERSONAL FINANCE ASSESSMENT

DATE:

SALARY	RENT EXPENSE/MORTGAGE
BUSINESS	UTILITIES EXPENSES Electric/Water/Telephone/Internet
OTHER SOURCES	FOOD
OTHER SOURCES	INSURANCE
TOTAL INCOME	INTEREST EXPENSE/INSURANCE
NET MONTHLY INCOME Total Income - Total Expenses	TOTAL EXPENSES

ASSETS

Particular	Amount

Savings:

Investment

Total Assets

Saving Habits:
_____
_____
_____

Short-term Financial Goals:
_____
_____
_____

DEBTS

Particular	Amount
Credit Card	
Credit Card	
Loans	
Loans	
Others	
Total Debt	

Spending Habits:
_____
_____
_____

Areas for Improvement:
_____
_____
_____

Long-term Financial Goals:
_____
_____
_____

PERSONAL FINANCE ASSESSMENT

DATE:	
SALARY	RENT EXPENSE/MORTGAGE
BUSINESS	UTILITIES EXPENSES Electric/Water/Telephone/Internet
OTHER SOURCES	FOOD
OTHER SOURCES	INSURANCE
TOTAL INCOME	INTEREST EXPENSE/INSURANCE
NET MONTHLY INCOME Total Income - Total Expenses	TOTAL EXPENSES

ASSETS

Particular	Amount

Savings: _____

Investment: _____

Total Assets

Saving Habits:
_____
_____
_____

Short-term Financial Goals:
_____
_____
_____

DEBTS

Particular	Amount
Credit Card	
Credit Card	
Loans	
Loans	
Others	
Total Debt	

Spending Habits:
_____
_____
_____

Areas for Improvement:
_____
_____
_____

Long-term Financial Goals:
_____
_____
_____

PERSONAL FINANCE ASSESSMENT

DATE:

SALARY		RENT EXPENSE/MORTGAGE	
BUSINESS		UTILITIES EXPENSES Electric/Water/Telephone/Internet	
OTHER SOURCES		FOOD	
OTHER SOURCES		INSURANCE	
TOTAL INCOME		INTEREST EXPENSE/INSURANCE	
NET MONTHLY INCOME Total Income - Total Expenses		TOTAL EXPENSES	

ASSETS

Particular	Amount
Savings:	
Investment	
Total Assets	

Saving Habits:

Short-term Financial Goals:

DEBTS

Particular	Amount
Credit Card	
Credit Card	
Loans	
Loans	
Others	
Total Debt	

Spending Habits:

Areas for Improvement:

Long-term Financial Goals:

PERSONAL FINANCE ASSESSMENT

DATE:	

SALARY	
BUSINESS	
OTHER SOURCES	
OTHER SOURCES	
TOTAL INCOME	
NET MONTHLY INCOME Total Income - Total Expenses	

RENT EXPENSE/MORTGAGE	
UTILITIES EXPENSES Electric/Water/Telephone/Internet	
FOOD	
INSURANCE	
INTEREST EXPENSE/INSURANCE	
TOTAL EXPENSES	

ASSETS

Particular	Amount
Savings:	
Investment	
Total Assets	

DEBTS

Particular	Amount
Credit Card	
Credit Card	
Loans	
Loans	
Others	
Total Debt	

Spending Habits:

Saving Habits:

Areas for Improvement:

Short-term Financial Goals:

Long-term Financial Goals:

PERSONAL FINANCE ASSESSMENT

DATE:	
SALARY	RENT EXPENSE/MORTGAGE
BUSINESS	UTILITIES EXPENSES Electric/Water/Telephone/Internet
OTHER SOURCES	FOOD
OTHER SOURCES	INSURANCE
TOTAL INCOME	INTEREST EXPENSE/INSURANCE
NET MONTHLY INCOME Total Income - Total Expenses	TOTAL EXPENSES

ASSETS

Particular	Amount

Savings:

Investment

Total Assets

Saving Habits:

Short-term Financial Goals:

DEBTS

Particular	Amount
Credit Card	
Credit Card	
Loans	
Loans	
Others	
Total Debt	

Spending Habits:

Areas for Improvement:

Long-term Financial Goals:

PERSONAL FINANCE ASSESSMENT

DATE:

SALARY	RENT EXPENSE/MORTGAGE
BUSINESS	UTILITIES EXPENSES Electric/Water/Telephone/Internet
OTHER SOURCES	FOOD
OTHER SOURCES	INSURANCE
TOTAL INCOME	INTEREST EXPENSE/INSURANCE
	TOTAL EXPENSES

NET MONTHLY INCOME
Total Income - Total Expenses

ASSETS

Particular	Amount

Savings:

Investment

Total Assets

Saving Habits:

DEBTS

Particular	Amount
Credit Card	
Credit Card	
Loans	
Loans	
Others	
Total Debt	

Spending Habits:

Areas for Improvement:

Short-term Financial Goals:

Long-term Financial Goals:

PERSONAL FINANCE ASSESSMENT

DATE:	
SALARY	RENT EXPENSE/MORTGAGE
BUSINESS	UTILITIES EXPENSES Electric/Water/Telephone/Internet
OTHER SOURCES	FOOD
OTHER SOURCES	INSURANCE
TOTAL INCOME	INTEREST EXPENSE/INSURANCE
NET MONTHLY INCOME Total Income - Total Expenses	TOTAL EXPENSES

ASSETS

Particular	Amount

Savings:

Investment

Total Assets

Saving Habits:

Short-term Financial Goals:

DEBTS

Particular	Amount
Credit Card	
Credit Card	
Loans	
Loans	
Others	
Total Debt	

Spending Habits:

Areas for Improvement:

Long-term Financial Goals:

PERSONAL FINANCE ASSESSMENT

DATE:	
SALARY	RENT EXPENSE/MORTGAGE
BUSINESS	UTILITIES EXPENSES Electric/Water/Telephone/Internet
OTHER SOURCES	FOOD
OTHER SOURCES	INSURANCE
TOTAL INCOME	INTEREST EXPENSE/INSURANCE
NET MONTHLY INCOME Total Income - Total Expenses	TOTAL EXPENSES

ASSETS

Particular	Amount

Savings:

Investment

Total Assets

Saving Habits:

Short-term Financial Goals:

DEBTS

Particular	Amount
Credit Card	
Credit Card	
Loans	
Loans	
Others	
Total Debt	

Spending Habits:

Areas for Improvement:

Long-term Financial Goals:

Part 4: Habits and Mindset

Welcome to the Habits and Mindset section of the P.A.T.H. Playbook. In this section, we will focus on developing positive financial habits and cultivating a positive mindset towards money.

It is important to recognize that financial success is not just about making more money. It's also about developing the right mindset and habits that will support your financial goals. By adopting positive financial habits and cultivating a positive mindset towards money, you can achieve not only financial success but also personal growth and fulfillment.

In this section, we will cover topics such as saving money, avoiding debt, and surrounding yourself with supportive people who share your financial goals and values. We will also explore the importance of mindset, including how to identify and overcome limiting beliefs, practice gratitude and affirmations, and use visualization to create a positive relationship with money.

By developing positive habits and mindset towards money, you will not only achieve financial success but also experience a greater sense of control, security, and fulfillment in your life. Let's dive in and start cultivating a positive relationship with money!

Overview of the Habits and Mindset section:

This part of the playbook aims to:

1. Develop Positive Financial Habits
   Learn how to cultivate positive financial habits such as saving money, avoiding debt, and creating a budget. These habits will help you achieve financial stability and live a financially successful life.
2. Cultivate a Positive Mindset Towards Money
   A positive mindset towards money is essential for achieving financial success. Learn how to cultivate a growth mindset, overcome limiting beliefs, and practice gratitude, affirmations, and visualization to create a positive relationship with money.
3. Surround Yourself with Supportive People
   Building a supportive community is essential for achieving your financial goals. Surround yourself with people who share your financial goals and values, and who will encourage and support you on your financial journey.

By working on your habits and mindset towards money, you can create a strong foundation for achieving financial freedom and success. The Habits and Mindset section of the PATH journal provides practical tools and exercises to help you cultivate positive financial habits and a growth mindset toward money.

Develop Positive Financial Habits:

Developing positive financial habits is an essential part of achieving financial stability and success. It's not just about making more money, but also about managing your finances wisely and making smart decisions that can help you reach your financial goals. In this section of the P.A.T.H.

Playbook, we will explore some of the most important financial habits that you should develop in order to achieve financial success.

- Saving Money
    - The first habit to develop is saving money. Saving money is crucial for building wealth, creating a financial cushion for emergencies, and achieving your long-term financial goals.
- Avoiding Debt
    - Another important habit to cultivate is avoiding debt. Debt can be a major obstacle to financial success, as it can drain your resources, create stress and anxiety, and limit your options.
- Creating a budget
    - Creating a budget is also an important habit to develop. A budget is a powerful tool for managing your finances and achieving your financial goals. We will guide you through the process of creating a budget that works for you, taking into account your income, expenses, and financial goals.

By developing positive financial habits and cultivating a growth mindset towards money, you can achieve financial stability and success. The Habits and Mindset section of the P.A.T.H. Playbook is designed to provide you with the tools and strategies you need to achieve your financial goals and live a financially successful life.

Cultivate a Positive Mindset Toward Money

Developing a positive mindset towards money is an essential part of achieving financial freedom. When you have a positive attitude towards money, you are more likely to attract abundance into your life and take the necessary steps towards achieving your financial goals.

- Cultivate a Growth Mindset
    - A growth mindset is the belief that you can develop your abilities and intelligence through hard work, dedication, and perseverance. With a growth mindset, you see challenges as opportunities for growth and learning, rather than obstacles to overcome.
    - To cultivate a growth mindset towards money, focus on learning and improving your financial knowledge and skills. Take courses, read books, and seek out mentorship or coaching to improve your financial literacy and confidence.
- Overcome Limiting Beliefs
    - Limiting beliefs are negative thoughts and beliefs that hold you back from achieving your goals. Common limiting beliefs around money include beliefs such as "money is the root of all evil" or "I'll never be rich."
    - To overcome limiting beliefs, identify them and challenge them with positive affirmations and evidence to the contrary. Replace negative self-talk with positive, empowering beliefs about money and your ability to achieve financial success.
- Practice Gratitude

- Practicing gratitude is a powerful way to cultivate a positive mindset towards money. When you focus on the abundance and blessings in your life, you attract more of the same into your life.
- To practice gratitude, write down three things you are grateful for each day related to your finances. This could be anything from having a stable job to receiving unexpected money. By focusing on the positive aspects of your financial situation, you will attract more abundance into your life.

- Use Positive Affirmations and Visualization
    - Positive affirmations and visualization are powerful tools for creating a positive mindset toward money. Affirmations are positive statements that you repeat to yourself, such as "I am worthy of financial abundance." Visualization is the process of imagining yourself already having achieved your financial goals.
    - To use positive affirmations and visualization, write down your financial goals and create affirmations that support them. For example, if your goal is to save $10,000, create an affirmation such as "I am so grateful to have saved $10,000 and feel proud of my financial discipline." Visualize yourself having achieved your financial goals and feel the positive emotions associated with that achievement.

In conclusion, cultivating a positive mindset toward money is essential for achieving financial success. By developing a growth mindset, overcoming limiting beliefs, practicing gratitude, and using positive affirmations and visualization, you can create a positive relationship with money and attract abundance into your life.

Surrounding Yourself with Supportive People

Finally, we will discuss the importance of surrounding yourself with supportive people who share your financial goals and values. Having a supportive network can provide you with encouragement, accountability, and motivation on your financial journey.

Achieving financial success is not a solo journey. It requires a supportive network of family, friends, and mentors who share your financial goals and values.

Surrounding yourself with positive people who uplift and inspire you is crucial in your financial journey. These people can provide you with support, guidance, and encouragement during tough times, and can also help keep you accountable to your financial goals.

It's important to identify the people in your life who have a positive influence on your finances and spend more time with them. These individuals can be successful entrepreneurs, investors, or financial advisors who can share their experience and knowledge with you.

On the other hand, it's equally important to distance yourself from negative people who drain your energy and discourage you from pursuing your financial goals. These people can be toxic and may hinder your financial success.

Remember that the people you surround yourself with can have a significant impact on your mindset, habits, and overall financial well-being. Seek out positive influences and surround yourself with people who will support and challenge you to be the best version of yourself

"Rich people have small TVs and big libraries, and poor people have small libraries and big TVs." - Zig Ziglar

Overcoming Limited Beliefs

	Limiting Beliefs	Overcoming Statements
1		
2		
3		
4		
5		
6		
7		

Guide:
List down your limiting beliefs which hinder your growth. Think of the negative Beliefs can have a significant impact on how you approach money and finances. In this exercise, you will identify any limiting beliefs that might be affecting your financial decisions and replace them with positive affirmations.

Begin by writing on the two columns. In the first column, write down any negative beliefs you have about money, such as "money is the root of all evil" or "I will never be able to get out of debt." It's important to be honest with yourself and write down any negative beliefs, even if they feel uncomfortable.

In the second column, write down a positive affirmation or statement that counters each negative belief. For example, if you wrote down "I will never be able to get out of debt," your positive affirmation could be "I am taking steps every day to become debt-free and financially independent." The goal of this exercise is to replace negative thoughts with positive ones that will help you achieve your financial goals.

Once you have completed your list of negative beliefs and positive affirmations, read through them regularly, especially when you notice negative thoughts creeping in. This will help reprogram your mindset and strengthen your positive beliefs about money and finances.

Remember that developing a positive mindset towards money is a process, and it takes time and effort. But with consistent practice and a willingness to change your beliefs, you can develop a healthy relationship with money and achieve financial success.

Positive Affirmations

Guide:
- Find a quiet and comfortable place where you can focus on writing positive affirmations.
- Start by writing down positive affirmations or statements. For example, "I am capable of saving money and creating wealth.", "I am financially free."
- Make sure your affirmations are specific, positive, and present tense. Write them as if they are already true and happening in your life.
- Repeat your positive affirmations daily, either by reading them aloud or silently. Visualize yourself living a life where your positive affirmations are true.
- Update your affirmations as you grow and progress in your financial journey.
- Celebrate your wins and acknowledge areas where you can continue to grow and improve.
- Remember, positive affirmations are a powerful tool for reprogramming your mindset and beliefs towards money and finances. By practicing them regularly, you can attract more abundance and financial success into your life.

"The only way to become rich is to stand in the shoes of the rich and do what the rich do." - T. Harv Eker

Gratitude Journal

_____
_____
_____
_____
_____
_____
_____
_____

Guide:
- This is your dedicated space for your gratitude practice.
- Set a time: Decide on a specific time each day that you will dedicate to writing in your gratitude journal. It could be in the morning, at night, or during a break in the day. The important thing is to make it a consistent habit.
- Reflect on your day: Take a few minutes to reflect on your day and think about the things you are grateful for. Consider both big and small things, from the people in your life to a beautiful sunset.
- Write it down: Write down your gratitude list in your journal. Try to be specific and descriptive about what you are grateful for. Instead of just writing "I'm grateful for my family," you could write "I'm grateful for the way my mom always makes time to listen to me."
- Add details: Add details to your gratitude list. What about the thing you are grateful for makes you feel happy or fulfilled? How does it make your life better?
- Keep it up: Make your gratitude journal a daily practice. Even if you don't feel particularly grateful one day, try to find at least one thing that you can appreciate.

Remember, the purpose of a gratitude journal is to help shift your focus from what you don't have to what you do have. By making a conscious effort to practice gratitude each day, you may find that you feel more positive and content overall.

Gratitude Journal

Gratitude Journal

Gratitude Journal

Gratitude Journal

Gratitude Journal

Gratitude Journal

Gratitude Journal

Gratitude Journal

Gratitude Journal

Gratitude Journal

Gratitude Journal

Gratitude Journal

Gratitude Journal

Gratitude Journal

Gratitude Journal

Gratitude Journal

Gratitude Journal

Gratitude Journal

"Money is a terrible master but an excellent servant." - P.T. Barnum

Notes

Notes

Notes

Notes

Notes

Notes

Notes

Notes

Notes

Notes

Notes

"It's not about how much money you make, but how much money you keep, how hard it works for you, and how many generations you keep it for." - Robert Kiyosaki

Part 5: Bonus

This section of the PATH playbook provides additional resources and inspiration to support you on your financial journey. This section includes a list of recommended books, websites, podcasts, and other resources for further education and inspiration.

Additionally, this section includes motivational quotes and success stories to keep you inspired and motivated along the way. Reading about the experiences of others who have achieved financial freedom can help you stay focused on your goals and remind you that success is possible.

Recommended Resources

"The Total Money Makeover" by Dave Ramsey

"The Simple Path to Wealth" by JL Collins

"The Millionaire Next Door" by Thomas J. Stanley and William D. Danko

"Rich Dad Poor Dad" by Robert Kiyosaki.

Websites like Investopedia and NerdWallet offer valuable financial information and advice.

Other Resources

- Financial calculators: Provide links or instructions on how to use online financial calculators for budgeting, debt repayment, retirement planning, and other financial goals.
- Webinars and courses: Recommend webinars or courses that cover personal finance topics, such as investing, budgeting, and debt management. Some courses are available for free or at a low cost, while others may require an investment.
- Financial apps: Suggest mobile apps that can help with budgeting, tracking expenses, or investing. Many apps are free or low-cost and can be easily downloaded from app stores.
- Local resources: Include a list of local resources, such as financial advisors, credit counselors, and community organizations that offer financial education or assistance.

- Personal finance blogs or podcasts: Provide a list of personal finance blogs or podcasts that can offer additional insights and inspiration on managing money.
- Success stories: Feature success stories from people who have achieved financial freedom or made significant progress towards their financial goals. These stories can serve as motivation and inspiration for journal users.

Financial Calculators

Financial calculators are excellent tools for planning and managing your finances effectively. Here are some examples of online financial calculators you can use:

- Budget Calculator: This calculator helps you create a budget by estimating your monthly income and expenses. You can adjust your expenses and see how much you can save each month.
- Debt Repayment Calculator: This calculator helps you create a plan to pay off your debt by calculating the monthly payments and the time required to pay off the debt.
- Retirement Calculator: This calculator helps you estimate how much money you will need for retirement based on your current savings and expected retirement expenses.
- Savings Calculator: This calculator helps you determine how much money you need to save each month to reach your financial goals.

To use these calculators, you can search for them online and enter your financial information into the provided fields. You can also find calculators on financial websites or apps. Be sure to read the instructions carefully and enter accurate information to get the most accurate results.

Using financial calculators can help you make informed financial decisions and achieve your financial goals faster.

Popular Financial Apps

Popular financial apps that can help with budgeting, tracking expenses, or investing:

- Mint: This app helps you track your spending, create a budget, and monitor your investments.
- YNAB (You Need A Budget): This app helps you create a budget and stick to it, and it also provides financial education to help you make better money decisions.
- Acorns: This app helps you invest your spare change and offers retirement accounts.
- Robinhood: This app allows you to buy and sell stocks, ETFs, and cryptocurrencies with no commission fees.
- Personal Capital: This app helps you track your net worth, create a budget, and monitor your investments.
- PocketGuard: This app helps you track your spending, create a budget, and save money.
- Betterment: This app helps you invest in a diversified portfolio with no account minimums.
- Credit Karma: This app helps you monitor your credit score and provides free credit reports and monitoring.
- Stash: This app allows you to invest in stocks, ETFs, and other assets with as little as $5.
- Digit: This app helps you save money by analyzing your spending habits and automatically transferring small amounts to a savings account.

These apps can help you stay on top of your finances and make informed financial decisions.

Remember, achieving financial empowerment is a journey, not a destination. The PATH playbook is just one tool to help you on this journey. Use the bonus section to continue learning and stay motivated as you work towards your financial goals.

Dear reader,

Congratulations on your journey to use the P.A.T.H. Playbook for Financial Empowerment! You have taken the first step towards achieving your financial goals and building a better future for yourself.

Remember that the journey towards financial freedom is not a sprint, but a marathon. It takes time, effort, and patience. But with the tools and strategies you have learned from this playbook, you are well on your way to success.

Continue to prioritize your financial health by regularly reviewing your progress, adjusting your goals and plans as needed, and cultivating positive financial habits and mindset. And always remember the importance of gratitude and giving back as you achieve your financial goals.

We hope that this playbook has provided you with the guidance, structure, and inspiration you need to achieve financial empowerment. May you continue to prosper and grow on your financial journey.

Best wishes,

Lee

About the Author

Lee Vincent is a successful entrepreneur who has founded and led multiple successful businesses in various industries such as logistics, finance, and commercial services. Through her experience, she has gained extensive knowledge in the areas of financial management, goal setting, and personal development.

As an author, Lee has published several motivational books that have inspired and empowered readers to take control of their lives and achieve their goals. Her writing style is influenced by her background in education, which has allowed her to create journals and planners that are easy to understand and practical to use.

The P.A.T.H. Playbook is the result of Lee's passion for helping people achieve financial stability and success. With her expertise in money management and mindset, she has formulated a comprehensive guide that can help anyone, regardless of their financial situation, to take control of their finances and achieve their goals.

Lee's mission is to empower and inspire people to live their best lives by providing them with the tools and resources they need to succeed. Through her writing and coaching, she has helped countless individuals overcome their limiting beliefs, develop positive habits, and create a life of abundance and fulfillment.

In addition to her entrepreneurial pursuits and writing, Lee is also a dedicated philanthropist and actively supports various charitable organizations. She believes in giving back to the community and using her success to make a positive impact on the world. To top them all, Lee is a self-confessed environmentalist who incorporates sustainability to her business materials and processes.

Overall, Lee Vincent is a talented and passionate author, entrepreneur, and philanthropist who has dedicated her life to helping others achieve their goals and live their best lives.

"The difference between rich and poor is that the rich invest their money and spend what is left, while the poor spend their money and invest what is left." - Jim Rohn

Made in the USA
Columbia, SC
21 April 2023